MAPPING COASTS

Louise Spilsbury

www.raintreepublishers.co.uk
Visit our website to find out more information about Raintree books.

To order:
☎ Phone 0845 6044371
🖹 Fax +44 (0) 1865 312263
🖳 Email myorders@raintreepublishers.co.uk

Customers from outside the UK please telephone +44 1865 312262

First published in Great Britain by Heinemann Library, Halley Court, Jordan Hill, Oxford OX2 8EJ, part of Harcourt Education.
Heinemann is a registered trademark of Harcourt Education Ltd.

© Harcourt Education Ltd 2005
First published in paperback in 2006
The moral right of the proprietor has been asserted.

Editorial: Lucy Thunder and Harriet Milles
Design: Ron Kamen and Celia Jones
Illustrations: Barry Atkinson, Darren Lingard and Jeff Edwards
Picture Research: Melissa Allison and Beatrice Ray
Production: Camilla Smith

Originated by Repro Multi Warna
Printed and bound in China by Leo Paper Group

The paper used to print this book comes from sustainable resources.

ISBN 978 0 431 01323 7 (hardback)
10
10 9 8 7 6 5 4 3 2
ISBN 978 0 431 01328 2 (paperback)
10 09 08 07 06
10 9 8 7 6 5 4 3 2 1

British Library Cataloguing in Publication Data

Spilsbury, Louise
(Mapping the UK). – Mapping Coasts
526'.09146

A full catalogue record for this book is available from the British Library.

Acknowledgements
The Publishers would like to thank the following for permission to reproduce photographs: ©CollinsBartholomew, 2005 p. 20; Alamy Images pp. 7, 22; Antarctic Royalty-free p. 24 (Arctic coast); Blackpool Pleasure Beach p. 5; Corbis/Royalty-free pp. 10 (sand, shingle), 14, 25 (palm trees, Monte Carlo, surfer), 26; GetMapping p. 8; Getty Images/Photodisc p. 24 (Oregon coast); Harcourt Education Ltd/Peter Evans pp. 6, 10 (cliffs), 12, 19; istockphoto.com pp. 10 (dunes), 17b; Jane Hance p. 10 (picnic table, caravan, camp site); Lonely Planet Images p. 7; Margaret Mackintosh p. 10 (groynes); Reproduced by permission of Ordnance Survey on behalf of The Controller of Her Majesty's Stationery Office, © Crown Copyright 100000230 pp. 13, 15, 17t, 19, 21; Simmons Aerofilms pp. 13, 18; Skyscan Photolibrary p. 15; TLFE p.10 (lighthouse).

Cover photograph of cliffs on the Ulster coast near Ballycastle, reproduced with permission of Harcourt Education Ltd/Peter Evans. Section of Ordnance Survey map reproduced by permission of Ordnance Survey of Northern Ireland.

The Publishers would like to thank Dr Margaret Mackintosh, Honorary Editor of *Primary Geographer*, for her assistance in the preparation of this book.

Every effort has been made to contact copyright holders of any material reproduced in this book. Any omissions will be rectified in subsequent printings if notice is given to the Publishers.

Disclaimer
All the Internet addresses (URLs) given in this book were valid at the time of going to press. However, due to the dynamic nature of the Internet, some addresses may have changed, or sites may have changed or ceased to exist since publication. While the author and Publishers regret any inconvenience this may cause readers, no responsibility for any such changes can be accepted by either author or the Publishers.

Contents

Words appearing in the text in bold, **like this**, are explained in the Glossary.

> ▶ Look out for this symbol!
> When you see it next to a
> question, you will find the
> answer on page 29.

What are maps?

Have you ever been to the seaside? If so, perhaps you or your family or friends used a map to find the way there. A map is a flat drawing of a place as it would be seen from above. Maps show us an **aerial** view of a landscape, as if we were looking down on it from the sky.

I-spy

Some people get confused when they look at maps because they find it hard to imagine what a place looks like from above. To help you see the world as maps do, look at different objects from the side and then from above. You could also think about how the rooms in your house would look from above. Perhaps you could try making a sketch map of a room, like the map of a beach resort below.

Hi there! I'm Carta. Pack your surfboard and your sunscreen and stick with me as we explore coasts. Together we'll find out how useful and how much fun maps can be!

Can you see the café and the paddling pool in this sketch map? If you visited this beach, where would you go first?

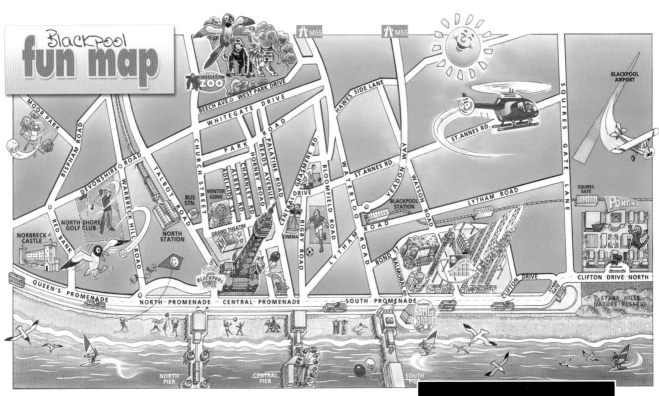

Leave it out!

There is not enough room on a map to show absolutely everything in a place, so mapmakers have to choose what to include and what to leave out. Unless it is a 'fun map' like the one above, a map usually only shows **permanent features** – the things that are always there. For instance, maps will show you the sand, sea, and rocks, but not the boats on the water or people sunbathing on the beach.

A coastal cruise

This book will help you find out about the different kinds of coasts around the UK – from sandy beaches to rocky **cliffs**. It also explains how maps can help you to discover lots of interesting information about coastal areas.

This is a pictorial 'fun map' of Blackpool. It shows an aerial view of the seafront, with little pictures of things tourists might want to visit. Pictorial maps are fun and easy to understand.

Looking at coasts

Coasts are the places where the land and sea meet. If you walked around the edge of the UK you would pass through many different kinds of coast.

Rocky shores

Day after day, powerful waves carrying sand and pebbles crash against the rocks on a coastline. They gradually wear the rocks away, and this is called **erosion**. Some coasts are made up of bands of hard and soft rock. Here the softer rock is eroded to form caves and **bays**. The harder rock is left jutting into the sea as a **headland**.

Cliffs are high, steep rock-faces. At the coast, they are carved by waves that erode the edge of the land.

Beaches

Over thousands of years, the chunks of eroded rock tumble against each other in the sea. They get broken up into smaller rocks, then smaller, rounded pebbles and eventually into grains of sand. Beaches are formed by **deposition** – when the pebbles and sand are washed up, or deposited, into bays or along shorelines.

Sandy beaches like this are created by waves washing sand on to the shore.

Estuaries and mudflats

Estuaries are places where rivers meet the sea. As rivers flow along their course, they erode mud and sand from the land and carry it along with them. Just before they meet the sea, rivers slow down and drop, or deposit, the mud and sand in the estuary. This forms areas of muddy land called mudflats.

The place where a river meets the sea at a coast is called a **mouth**. Can you see the mudflats along the sides of this river as it flows to the mouth?

7

Marking coasts on a map

To make maps of coastal areas, mapmakers use several sources of information. People called surveyors take careful measurements and notes about the location of things on the ground. Mapmakers also use **aerial** photographs taken by cameras in aeroplanes or **satellites**.

Looking at an aerial photograph

This aerial photo shows Barmouth, a seaside resort in Wales. Here the River Mawddach meets the sea. Can you spot the large sandy beach and the Barmouth Bridge across the river? You should also be able to see some fence-like barriers, called **groynes**, along the beach. People build groynes to prevent **longshore drift**. Longshore drift is when the sea washes sand and pebbles sideways along a beach and drags them away. Groynes trap the sand and stop the beach being moved along the coast, or lost in the sea.

This aerial photo of Barmouth looks straight down on the area from above.

Mapping Barmouth in Wales

The map below is a very simple sketch map of Barmouth beach drawn from the aerial photograph opposite. This map uses colours and shapes to show where different features are. Like real maps, it only shows a limited number of things and only the **permanent features**. The blue area is the river and the sea, and the yellow area is the sand. The buildings are shown in black and the land around is brown. Areas of woodland are green. The groynes are labelled and shown as black lines. You can use any aerial photos to make a map. Why don't you try drawing a simple sketch map like this one, using colours to show different features.

It's not just because beaches are good for holidays that people protect them with groynes. Beaches absorb some of the impact of the waves hitting a shore and slow the sea's erosion of the land.

Groynes

Barmouth Bridge

River Mawddach

Seaside symbols

Maps often cover quite a big area and show a large number of different features. It would be impossible to label every single thing on a map, so mapmakers use colours and symbols to represent things on the ground.

How do symbols work?

Symbols are simple pictures, shapes, lines, or even letters that represent real things. We see and use symbols every day. When a teacher gives you a star, it is a symbol to show that you have done good work! Maps use lots of symbols around coastal areas. Some represent natural features, such as mud or **sand dunes**. Other symbols show things that people have built on or by coasts, such as **groynes** or lighthouses.

These are some of the symbols used to represent coastal features on maps. When you draw a map, try to make up some of your own symbols!

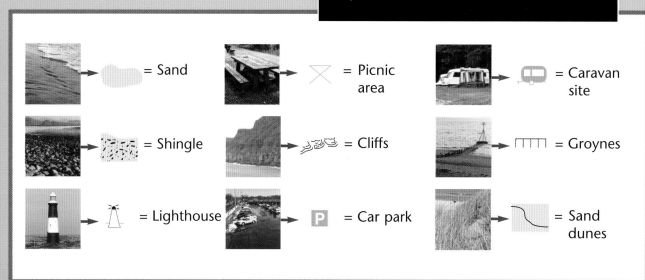

= Sand

= Picnic area

= Caravan site

= Shingle

= Cliffs

= Groynes

= Lighthouse

= Car park

= Sand dunes

Can you guess what some of the symbols on this map mean? If not, check out the map key. A map key is a list of the symbols used with an explanation of what they mean. A key helps you to unlock a map's secrets!

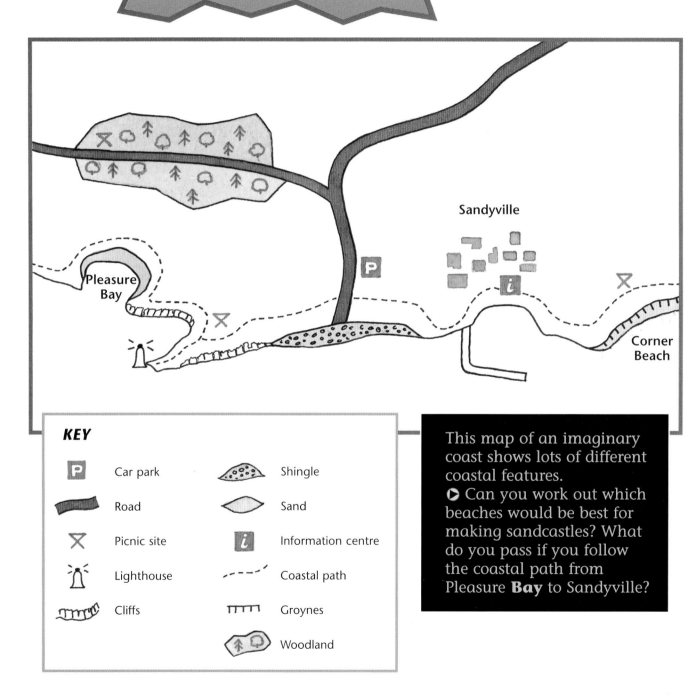

Pleasure Bay

Sandyville

Corner Beach

KEY

P	Car park	Shingle	Shingle
	Road	Sand	Sand
☓	Picnic site	i	Information centre
	Lighthouse	- - - -	Coastal path
	Cliffs	TTTTT	Groynes
			Woodland

This map of an imaginary coast shows lots of different coastal features.
▶ Can you work out which beaches would be best for making sandcastles? What do you pass if you follow the coastal path from Pleasure **Bay** to Sandyville?

Visit St Michael's Mount

St Michael's Mount is a pretty, rocky island with a castle perched on top. It is in Mounts Bay, near Marazion in Cornwall. Lots of tourists come to visit the castle on St Michael's Mount and enjoy the beaches at Marazion.

At high and low tides

An island is a piece of land surrounded by water. At high **tide**, St Michael's Mount is cut off from the mainland by water and you can only get to it by ferry boat. At low tide, the Mount is joined to the mainland by beach and a raised stone path called a causeway.

Twice a day in the UK, the tide comes in and flows out again. High tide is when the sea reaches its highest point up a coast; low tide is when it has flowed all the way out again.

This is St Michael's Mount at low tide. Can you see the causeway to the Mount here, and on the map opposite?

Take a look at this **aerial** photograph of St Michael's Mount at high tide. Can you make out the causeway under the water?

Mapping the Mount

Compare the photograph above with the **Ordnance Survey** map of the area (below). It should be easy to spot the island and the **harbour** walls, where boats go in and out. The map also tells us something very important about tides here. The blue line marked 'Mean Low Water' shows us how much of the land is covered by sea at low tide. The blue line marked 'Mean High Water' shows us that, at high tide, the sea water covers most of the sand at Marazion and cuts off St Michael's Mount from the mainland.

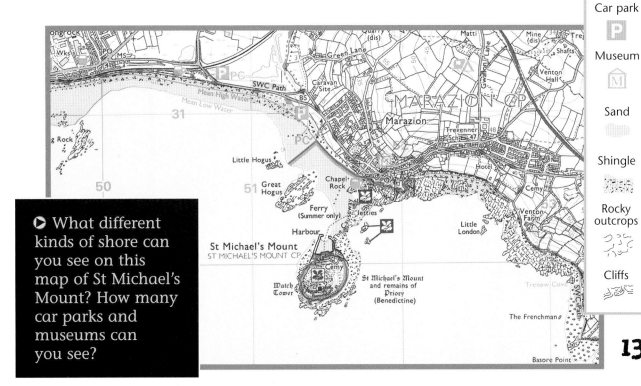

▷ What different kinds of shore can you see on this map of St Michael's Mount? How many car parks and museums can you see?

KEY

Car park

🅿

Museum

Ⓜ

Sand

Shingle

Rocky outcrops

Cliffs

13

Locating coasts

One way to locate coasts is using compass directions – north, east, south, and west. Most maps are drawn with north at the top, so you can describe where something is by giving its direction from something else. For example, in the sketch map below, Pleasure **Bay** is west of the car park and north of the lighthouse.

Getting to grip with grids

Many maps have sets of lines that form grid squares. These help you to locate things. In the map below, the lines going up (vertically) have different letters. The lines going across (horizontally) have numbers. A grid reference is the letter and number that mark a square. So, Pleasure Bay is in A,2 and the **shingle** beach is in C,1.

Try making up a rhyme like this to help you remember compass directions:

'**N**elly **E**lephant **S**urfs **W**ell'.

▶ Can you work out the grid reference for the car park? What coastal features do you find in E,1?

KEY

P	Car park		Shingle
	Road		Sand
☓	Picnic site	i	Information centre
	Lighthouse	- - - -	Coastal path
	Cliffs	⊓⊓⊓	Groynes
			Woodland

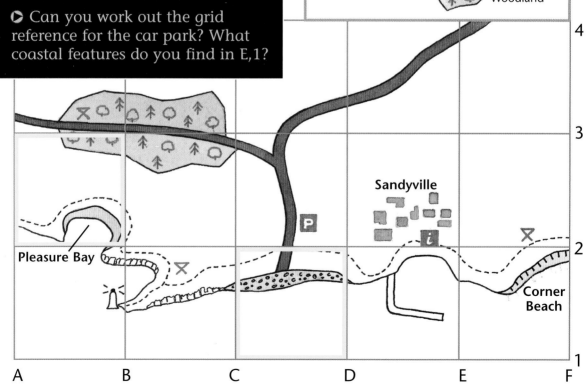

Pleasure Bay

Sandyville

Corner Beach

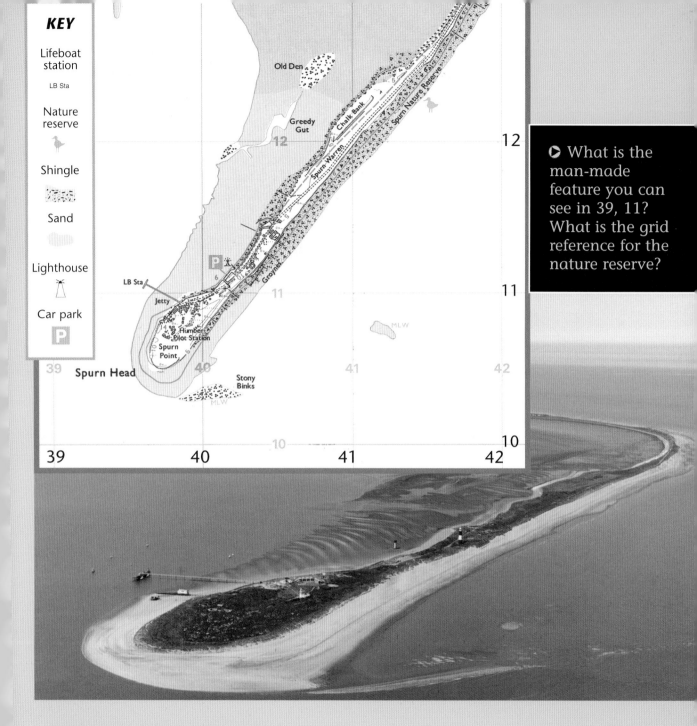

KEY

Lifeboat station

LB Sta

Nature reserve

Shingle

Sand

Lighthouse

Car park

P

▷ What is the man-made feature you can see in 39, 11? What is the grid reference for the nature reserve?

Map labels: Old Den, Greedy Gut, Chalk Bank, Spurn Nature Reserve, Spurn Warren, P, LB Sta, Jetty, Groyne, Humber Pilot Station, Spurn Point, Spurn Head, Stony Binks, MLW

Mapping Spurn Head

The photograph and map on this page show Spurn Head at the **mouth** of the Humber **Estuary** in Yorkshire. Spurn Head is a **spit** – a long ridge of sand and shingle that reaches out into the sea. **Ordnance Survey** maps use numbers for both the vertical and the horizontal grid lines. To read a grid reference, we give the number on the vertical line first and then the number on the horizontal line. (Remember this by the phrase: 'Along the corridor and up the stairs'!) So, the grid reference for Spurn Point at the end of Spurn Head is 39, 10 and for the car park it is 40, 11. (You can find more help with reading grid references on page 28.)

15

Cliffs and contours

Some coastlines slope gently down to the sea. Muddy shores and sandy beaches are usually quite flat, while **shingle** beaches are narrower and steeper. Along other coastlines there are steep or even vertical **cliffs** at the edge of the sea. How are all these highs and lows shown on maps?

Coastal contours

Alongside the cliff symbols on a coastal map, you will usually see thin brown lines. These are contour lines and they join up areas of land that are the same height in metres above sea level. The diagrams below give you an idea of how contours work.

Contours are tricky to understand! The main thing to remember is that on a steep slope the lines are drawn close together on a map, and on a gentler slope, the lines are farther apart.

The top part of this diagram shows the side view of a coastline with cliffs rising up from sea level. We have drawn lines up the slope of the cliff at every 10 metres. The bottom part of the diagram shows you how the contour lines of the cliff would look from above, on a map.

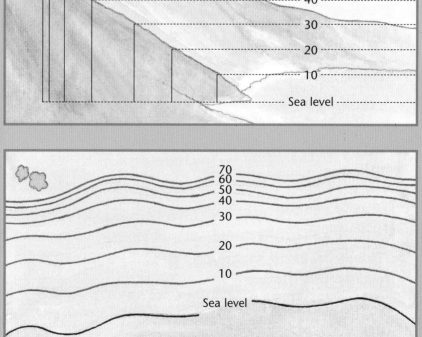

KEY

Shingle

Slopes

Rocky
outcrops

Sand

Cliff

High water
mark

Lighthouse

Mapping Beachy Head

The photograph below shows Beachy Head, the highest chalk cliff in England. Now compare the photograph with the **Ordnance Survey** map of the same area (above). The widely spaced contour lines on the cliff top tell us that the land slopes gently here. The edge of the cliff is shown by the cliff and slope symbols. Where the cliffs drop into the sea, there are a lot of contour lines very close together. That tells us that the cliff side here is *very* steep! The blue line where the contour lines end marks the bottom of the cliff, and shows us where the water comes up to at high **tide**.

▷ Using the map and the photograph, can you say what the land is like between the lighthouse and the cliff at low tide?

Explore Lulworth Cove and Durdle Door

Lulworth Cove and Durdle Door are possibly the most famous sights along the Dorset coastline in England. Below you can see a photograph of Lulworth Cove, a beautiful, nearly circular **bay**. Roughly 2 kilometres along the coast from Lulworth is Durdle Door. It is a huge archway of limestone rock, straddling the sea at the end of a **headland**. You can see a photograph of Durdle Door on the page opposite.

Opening the door!

Arches like Durdle Door are formed by **erosion**. Waves gradually wear a hole right through part of a **cliff** headland and create an arch. Eventually, erosion may make the arch of rock so thin and weak that the top falls into the sea, leaving just a lump of rock sticking out of the water. This is called a stack. One day in the future, Durdle Door may become a stack!

This is an **aerial** photograph of Lulworth Cove. The bay was formed by the sea eroding a weak point in the hard limestone cliffs, and then wearing away the soft rocks behind.

This arch of rock is called Durdle Door.

A Dorset walk

Using the map below, follow the coastal path from Durdle Door to Lulworth Cove. Answer these questions using your map skills:

▶ What is the name of the bay to the east of Durdle Door? Use the symbol key to say what kind of beach makes up this bay – sand, **shingle** or a mix of both?

▶ What do the closely-spaced contour lines at the back of Lulworth Cove tell us about these cliffs?

On the map you cannot see the arch of Durdle Door because we are looking down on it from above – but grid references can help you to find it! Durdle Door is at grid reference 80,80.

▶ What is the grid reference for Lulworth Cove?

KEY

Coastal path

Tourist feature

Telephone

Cliffs

Shingle

Sand

Caravan park

Camp site

19

A sense of scale

One of the main differences you will notice about maps is their scale. 'Scale models' are small versions of the real thing – like a toy car or a doll's house. Features and places also have to be 'scaled down' to fit on a map.

The secret of scales

A map's scale tells us exactly how much smaller things are on a map compared to real life. For example, a 1:25 000 scale map means that 1 centimetre on the map is equal to 25,000 centimetres (or 250 metres) in real life. So, if a beach were 10 centimetres long on a map it would be 2,500 metres (or 2.5 kilometres) long in real life. A map's scale is usually shown on a scale bar. You can see scale bars on the maps on these pages.

This is a small-scale map of the north Devon coast and Lundy Island. It mainly shows the towns and villages and the roads that link them up. Drivers might use this map to find the quickest way to Bideford. From there it is a short ferry ride to Lundy Island.

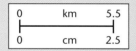

0	km	5.5
0	cm	2.5

© Collins 2005

Work it out

Lundy is a small island off the coast of North Devon. If you visit the island you might see seals, puffins and ponies. On the right is a large-scale map that shows the whole of Lundy in a lot of detail. You would use this map if you wanted to go walking on the island.

Grid squares also help with measuring distance. On an **Ordnance Survey** map each side of a grid square always represents 1 kilometre. By counting grid squares you can work out distances, too.

A large-scale map shows a fairly small area of land in a lot of detail. A small-scale map shows a bigger area of land but in less detail. We have put colour 'spotlights' on some of the maps in this book. These are to help you find places.

This is a large-scale map of Lundy Island. Each grid line on this map measures 4 centimetres and equals 1 kilometre in real life. ◐ Can you work out roughly how far it is from the camp site on the south of the island to North East Point?

Coasts of the UK

Coastlines are always changing. The coastline of the British Isles did not always look as it does today. In fact, long ago you would have been able to walk over to France, rather than having to fly or take a ferry across the water!

Around 20,000 years ago, during the Ice Age, the level of the sea was much lower and the British Isles were joined to the rest of Europe. Then, about 10,000 years ago, the ice that covered the land melted. The amount of water in the sea increased and sea levels rose. The low-lying land between Europe and the British Isles was flooded with water, separating the two areas. This is now called the English Channel.

The British Isles is made up of one very big island (Great Britain) and many much smaller ones. Altogether there are over 18,000 kilometres of coastline around the British Isles!

This is a photograph of the British Isles, taken from a camera on a **satellite** circling the Earth in space. The lighter areas around the coast show where the land slopes into the sea.

This map of the UK shows the areas that have won Blue Flag awards for clean beaches.

Making UK maps

Mapmakers use satellite pictures like the one opposite to make many different kinds of maps. The map above shows where to find some of the cleanest beaches in the UK. Parts of the UK coastline are **polluted** by litter, oil spills from ships, and **sewage** which flows out of our drains. Pollution can cause illness or injury to people, and to the millions of plants and animals that live on the coast and in the sea.

Going global

There are a huge variety of coastlines around the world. In some places, cities are built right at the edge of the sea. At the South Pole in Antarctica, the land is buried deep under layers of ice that extend into the sea. The coastline is white and bare, except for the penguins living there. On **tropical** shores, palm trees often fringe sandy beaches. In spite of their differences, all the coastlines of the world are affected and shaped by the power of the oceans and seas.

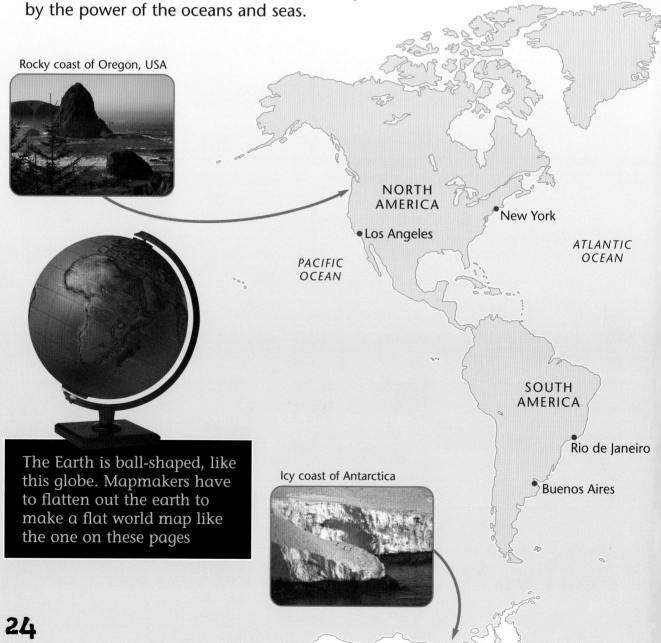

Rocky coast of Oregon, USA

The Earth is ball-shaped, like this globe. Mapmakers have to flatten out the earth to make a flat world map like the one on these pages

Icy coast of Antarctica

NORTH
AMERICA

● New York

● Los Angeles

PACIFIC
OCEAN

ATLANTIC
OCEAN

SOUTH
AMERICA

● Rio de Janeiro

● Buenos Aires

World coasts under threat

Some stretches of the world's coastline are disappearing under the sea. Many scientists believe that this is happening because the world's climate is getting warmer. The increased warmth is making some of the ice at the North and South Poles gradually melt into the sea. If sea levels continue to rise, some low-lying coastlines and islands of the world will find themselves permanently under water in the future.

Eight of the world's largest cities are by the coast. These are Buenos Aires, Kolkata, Lagos, Los Angeles, New York, Rio de Janeiro, Shanghai and Tokyo. Can you find these cities on a globe?

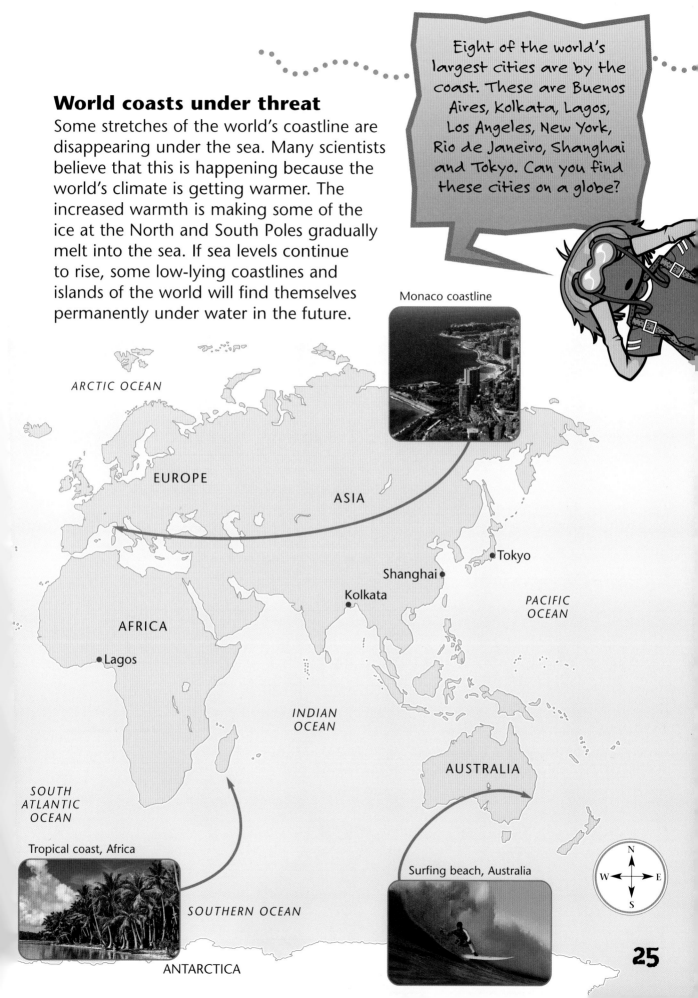

Monaco coastline

ARCTIC OCEAN

EUROPE

ASIA

AFRICA

• Lagos

• Kolkata

Shanghai •

• Tokyo

PACIFIC OCEAN

INDIAN OCEAN

SOUTH ATLANTIC OCEAN

Tropical coast, Africa

AUSTRALIA

Surfing beach, Australia

SOUTHERN OCEAN

ANTARCTICA

N
W E
S

Treasure hunt!

Be a pirate for a day! Set off in a pirate ship and find a fortune by following the trail around the map opposite. If you answer the questions correctly, you will collect eight letters – one from each island. Then put these letters together to make a word – and find out what the treasure is!

1 Starting from grid reference 15, 36, sail the ship north for 2 kilometres to reach an island (use the grid lines to work out this distance). Note down the first letter of the name of the **bay** on the west of the island.

2 Your crew is thirsty. You sail to the island where there is a river so they can get fresh water to drink. What is the name of the coastal feature that sticks out into the sea on the east of this island? (You could turn back to page 15 to remind yourself!) Write down the third letter of your answer.

3 Now the crew are hungry. You sail north to the island with an inn. What do you see in the bay on the west of this island ? Note the last letter of its name.

4 From the inn, catch a passing wind and sail due east, to the island with a long sandy beach. Take the first letter from the name of this island.

5 From here, sail to the island at grid reference 13, 38. You can see a wrecked ship to the northwest of this island. Note down the first letter of the shipwreck's name.

6 Now sail 3 kilometres eastwards, to an island with a lighthouse. Write down the third letter of this island's name.

7 Sail in a south-westerly direction to the island at grid reference 14, 33. Take the first letter from the name of the pirates' hideout here.

8 You have nearly made it! Sail northeast to a small island just 1 kilometre away. The treasure is buried in the middle of this island, and X marks the spot. Take the first letter from the name of the marsh that you have to walk through to get there.

Check out your answers on page 29 to see if you found the right treasure!

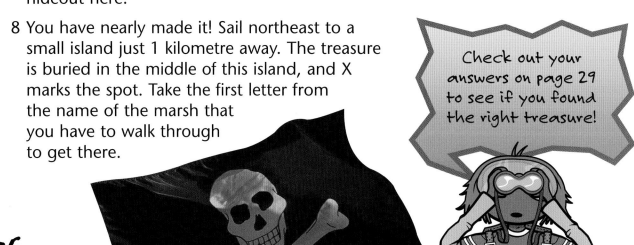

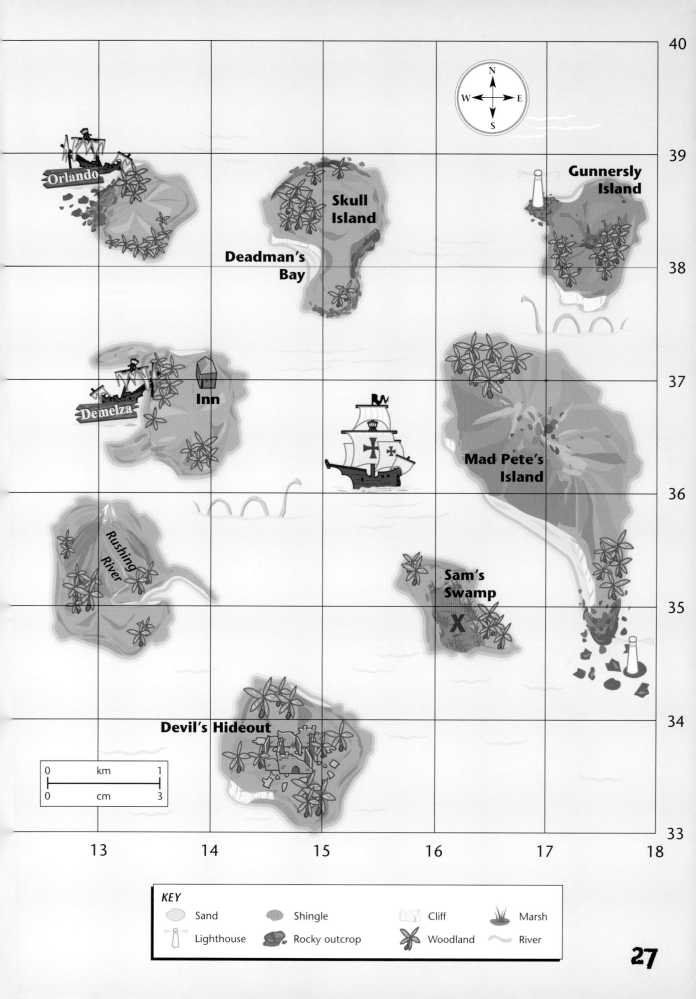

Quick-stop map skills

What are symbols?

Map symbols are pictures, letters, shapes, lines or patterns that represent different features, such as rivers and roads. Map keys show what the symbols stand for.

Key

 = Picnic area   = Caravan site

How can I measure distances?

On **Ordnance Survey** maps, each grid square represents 1 kilometre, so you can roughly judge distance by counting grid squares.

What are grid references?

Grid references are numbers that locate a particular square on a map. To give a grid reference, you give the number on the vertical lines first and then the number on the horizontal lines. ('Along the corridor and up the stairs.')

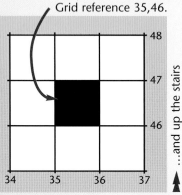

Grid reference 35,46.

...and up the stairs

Along the corridor…

How does scale work?

A map scale tells you how much smaller a feature is on a map than it is in real life. Everything on a map is scaled down in size. On a 1:25 000 scale map things are 25,000 times smaller than real life.

How are slopes shown on a map?

Maps show slopes by using shaded colours, contour lines, or **gradient** arrows. Gradient arrows look like this >>>. The more arrows, the steeper the slope. Contour lines join up areas of land that are the same height above sea level. When contour lines are close together the slope is steep. When contour lines are spaced out, the land is flatter. Numbers next to, or on the lines tell us the exact height of the land in metres.

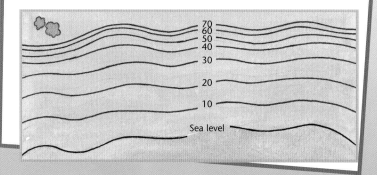

Map skills answers

Page 11: Pleasure **Bay** and Corner Beach would be the best beaches for making sandcastles because they are both sandy. If you follow the coastal path from Pleasure Bay to Sandyville, the symbols tell you that you will pass **cliffs**, a lighthouse, a picnic site, more cliffs, a **shingle** beach, a road, and a car park.

Page 13: On the map of St Michael's Mount we can see sandy and shingle shores along the mainland. We can also see two car parks and one museum.

Page 14: The grid reference for the car park is C,2. The coastal features in grid square E,1 are a coastal footpath, a sandy beach, and **groynes**.

Page 15: The man-made feature in grid reference 39,11 is the lifeboat station. The grid reference for the nature reserve is 41,12.

Page 17: The map tells us that the area between the lighthouse and the bottom of the cliff at Beachy Head is covered in rocks and a shingle beach.

Page 19: The name of the bay east of Durdle Door is St Oswald's Bay. The beach in this bay is a mix of sand and shingle. The closely-spaced contour lines tell us that the cliffs at the back of Lulworth Cove are very steep. The grid reference for Lulworth Cove is 82,79.

Page 21: The map tells us that it is about 4 kilometres from the camp site on the south of Lundy to North East Point at the top of the island.

Page 26: The treasure is DIAMONDS! 1 – D (Deadman's Bay); 2 – I (Spit); 3 – A (Demelza); 4 – M (Mad Pete's Island); 5 – O (Orlando); 6 – N (Gunnersly Island); 7 – D (Devil's Hideout); 8 – S (Swamp).

Glossary

aerial overhead, from the sky

bay inward curve in a coastline, where softer rock has been eroded

cliff high, steep rock-face found along the coastline

deposition drop or deposit material such as sand or shingle somewhere new

erosion when rocks are worn away, for example, by waves

estuary part of a river where it widens and meets the sea. In an estuary, fresh water from the river joins salt water from the sea.

gradient the steepness of a slope

groynes barriers that stop waves dragging sand or shingle off or along a beach

harbour place of shelter for ships

headland piece of land that juts out into the sea

longshore drift when waves drag sand and pebbles in a zigzag movement along a beach

mouth end of a river, where it flows into the sea

Ordnance Survey map-making organization that makes maps that cover the whole of the UK

permanent features things that are always in the same place. A car park is a permanent feature. A car parked there is not.

pollute when water, air or soil are made dirty or poisonous by people's and other waste

sand dunes mound or ridge of sand formed by the sea, usually at the back of a beach

satellite scientific object in space that can send out TV signals or take photographs

sewage human waste from household drains

shingle pebbles that have become smooth and round from being rolled against each other by water

spit ridge of land (made of sand, shingle or mud) sticking out into the sea. Formed by longshore drift.

tides the rise and fall of the sea along a shore, twice a day

tropical place in the Tropics, near the Equator, the hottest area on Earth

Find out more

Books

Wild Habitats: Coasts, Louise and Richard Spilsbury (Heinemann Library, 2004)

Philip's Junior School Atlas (4th edn), (Heinemann, Rigby, Ginn, 2003)

Websites

You can play games, get homework help and learn more about using Ordnance Survey maps on the Ordnance Survey Mapzone site:
www.ordnancesurvey.co.uk/mapzone

Find lots of information about beach pollution and climate change at the Environment Agency's Kids Zone:
www.environment-agency.gov.uk/fun

The BBC website has a 'litterhitter' game where you can have fun wiping out beach pollution! Try it at:
www.news.bbc.co.uk/cbbcnews/hi/static/games/whack/ cbbc_whack.stm

The National Trust owns and protects large stretches of UK coastline for everyone to enjoy. You can find out lots of facts about coasts and coastal wildlife, as well as the National Trust's work at:
www.nationaltrust.org.uk/coastline/kids

Have fun with maps in the future – you should never get lost again!

Index